A corncob, a feather, a small soccer ball,
A safety pin, a bike, and seven bears in all.

I spy three bottles, two starfish, a string,

A poodle, a pearl, a leaf, and a ring;

Four feathers, a button, a cork, a key,
A turtle, a coin, a 4, and a B.

I spy twelve arrows, two squares to be blue,
An exclamation point, two gerbils, a Q;

Two erasers, a bird, a yellow three,
Two question marks, and a pink apostrophe.

I spy eight flowerpots, a sign on a bone,

A pitchfork, a cage, and an old gramophone;

A rabbit, an octagon, six pin stripes, a 4,
A candelabra, a hanger, and a dollhouse door.

I spy a pencil, four blueberries, a bee,
And a winged pair of seeds from a maple tree;

The word IN twice, a bottle cap, a pin,
Two sunflower seeds, and a piece of snakeskin.

I spy a gas pump and Santa's green sack,
A football, hinged knees, and a milk bottle stack;

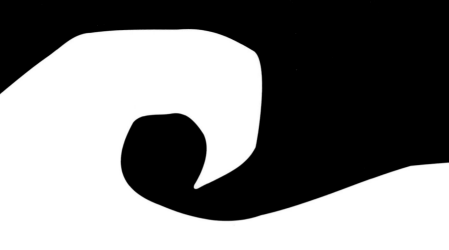

Tufted Puffin

One dark night he felt the tow.
The ocean called—it's time to go.

He fluttered down the hill alone,
And dove into the great unknown.

The plucky chick was six weeks old.
The waves were big, the water cold.

He swam and flew and swam some more,
Until he couldn't see the shore.

He felt at home! Content to be
Pelagic—born for life at sea.

Bald Eagle

The Eagle's wingspan, tip to tip, can measure seven feet.
Her beak is strong, her talons sharp, her eyesight can't be beat.

She uses all those qualities to rustle up her meals.
Fish and ducks are favorite prey, but when she can, she steals.

What a pirate! She can rob an Osprey of its prize,
Or pinch another Eagle's lunch despite protesting cries.

And every fall, a salmon feast. They come from miles around
To feed on fish in rivers swimming to their spawning ground.

Hundreds, even thousands gather for the salmon spree.
It's Eagles, Eagles everywhere—what a sight to see!

American Dipper

Dipper is named for her bobbing display,
Though just why she does it, no one can say.

She's plain—but she's an unusual bird.
How to describe her? Aquatic's the word!

Find her by streams that run tumbling and clear,
Look on the rocks for this plump little dear.

She hunts underwater for larvae and eggs,
Paddling her short stubby wings and pink legs.

Gripping the gravel and rocks as she goes,
With extra-long, super strong, grappling-hook toes.

Even in winter she's happy to dunk,
Iñupiats called her the "Old Woman Sunk."

Arctic Tern

Imagine for a moment you are winging through the sky,
Over miles of open sea, you fly, and fly, and fly....

That's the life of Arctic Tern, a graceful, streamlined bird,
Who migrates farther than them all—feathered, finned, or furred.

She nests along the northern coast, under midnight sun,
Laying eggs and raising chicks, until that job is done.

Then it's time to fly again, for distant southern clime,
To the bottom of the globe to rerun summertime.

She might live for thirty years, which puts her right on track,
To fly a lifetime distance to the moon three times and back!

Great Horned Owl

Owls are calling in the night,
Back and forth in starry light.

It's spring, and so the pair is set
To hoot their his-and-hers duet.

HOOO, hoo-hoo HOOO, she cries,
Hoo-hoo HOO, her mate replies.

They're hunting for an empty nest,
Hawk's or crow's would be the best.

HOO, she calls, *Hoo-hoo-HOO,*
This one's nice—you like it toooo?

HOOT, he answers. *Hoo-hoo-HOO,*
Yes, I love the woodsy view!

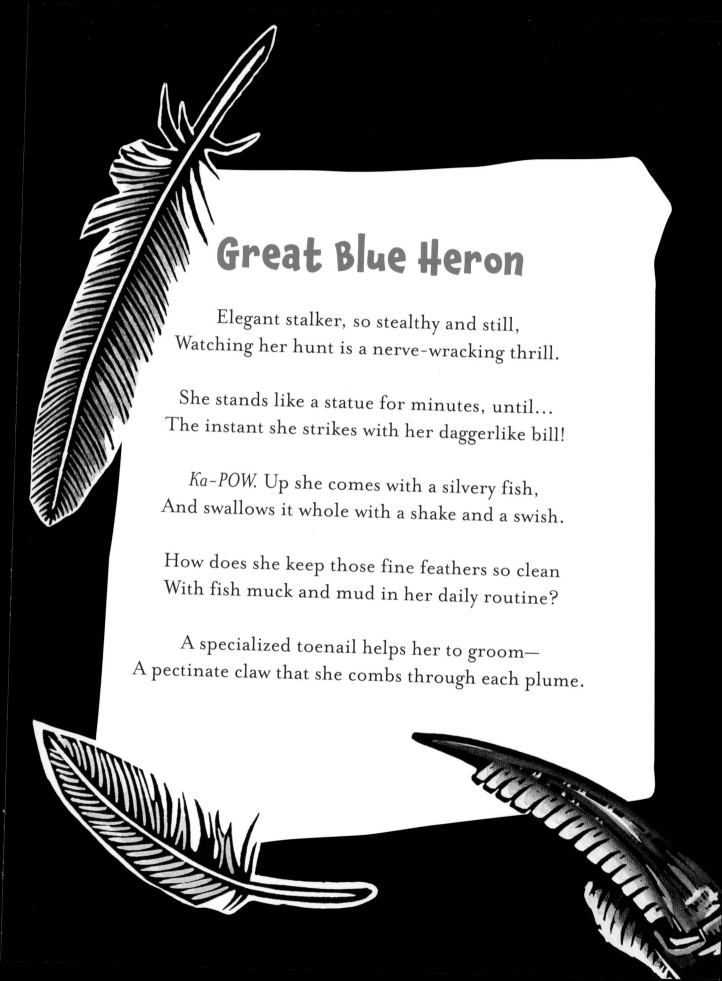

Great Blue Heron

Elegant stalker, so stealthy and still,
Watching her hunt is a nerve-wracking thrill.

She stands like a statue for minutes, until…
The instant she strikes with her daggerlike bill!

Ka-POW. Up she comes with a silvery fish,
And swallows it whole with a shake and a swish.

How does she keep those fine feathers so clean
With fish muck and mud in her daily routine?

A specialized toenail helps her to groom—
A pectinate claw that she combs through each plume.

KAWW

Common Raven

Raven played a starring role in tales told long ago.
No wonder that this cunning trickster always stole the show.

One look into his shiny eyes and you can plainly see
A clever corvid staring back with curiosity.

He's famous for his fun and games, in flight or on the ground,
Aerobatics, tug-of-war, and chasing wolves around.

Calling all the while—it's his expressive way of talking.
Every sound has meaning as he's *kaawing, quorking, klokking.*

Raven's telling stories through that chatty vocal mix
About his wild adventures and his wiliest of tricks.

yellow Warbler

He flits among the willow branches, seldom sitting still,
Gleaning insects off the leaves to eat his buggy fill.

At times he'll pause in his pursuit of beetles, ants, and bees
To chirp a cheerful tune that rings out sweetly through the trees.

He sings assorted songs at different hours of the day,
Each with special meaning that he wishes to convey.

A song might be to find a mate or share his morning mood.
There's one he sings out to his chicks—*I'm coming with your food!*

The Warbler can be hard to see, but plain as day to hear.
Learn to listen for his voice to "see" him with your ear.

Northern Flicker

Flicker is famous for drumming his bill
On tree trunks, a stovepipe, or wood windowsill.

This drumming is purely for show, not destruction.
His gouging and digging are saved for construction.

He'll carve out a cavity nest very neatly,
A foot or more down, hollowed completely.

Flicker is happy to build his own nest,
Then leave it behind for the next forest guest.

A Kestrel, a Screech Owl, a Goldeneye Duck,
Tree Swallows, Pygmy Owls—all are in luck.

As long as he hammers and chisels away,
They will have safe nesting places one day.

More About the Birds

Willow Ptarmigan
(Lagopus lagopus)
Year-round Alaska resident

As Alaska's State Bird, the Willow Ptarmigan has lots of adaptations to make it at home in the north country. For example, the Willow Ptarmigan sheds and grows new feathers (molts) almost continuously from early spring to late fall. Each new set of feathers grows in with colors that help camouflage the bird to hide it from predators. In summer, feathers are light to dark brown to match the tundra. In winter, feathers are white like the snow. Special feathers that work as snowshoes grow on the Ptarmigan's feet in winter, and its claws get longer to help it walk on ice. This built-in cold-weather gear comes in handy because the Willow Ptarmigan lives most of its life on the ground.

Willow Ptarmigan are the only members of the grouse family in which the male helps the female raise their young.

A group of Ptarmigan is called a *covey* or *invisibleness*.

Belted Kingfisher
(Megaceryle alcyon)
Year-round Alaska resident in Southeast and Southcentral Alaska; in Alaska's Interior they migrate south in the winter to find open water

Kingfishers rule when it comes to catching fish! With their ultra-streamlined bills, they can dive into the water with hardly a splash, catching a fish by surprise. And the big-headed birds see as well underwater as they do in the air.

Female Belted Kingfishers have a rufous breast band, making them one of the few birds where the female has more color than the male. Kingfishers, which always live near water, excavate burrow nests into streambanks. The male and female work together, taking turns digging with their bills and feet. The male helps care for the eggs and both parents feed the young. Belted Kingfishers have a call like a mechanical-sounding rattle, which they can make even with a mouthful of fish. There are over one hundred species of Kingfisher (including Australia's Kookaburra), but only the Belted Kingfisher lives in Alaska.

A group of Kingfishers is a *clique, crown,* or *rattle*.

Western Sandpiper
(Calidris mauri)
Alaska migrant

The entire population of Western Sandpipers migrates to Alaska every spring. The three million birds travel in waves from as far away as Central America, refueling along the way at food-rich stopovers like Alaska's Copper River Delta. There are about ten of these major "staging areas" on the route, and birds gather at each one by the thousands to gobble clams, grubs, crustaceans, and other goodies.

Bird watchers flock to staging areas along the Pacific Coast to gaze in wonder at the spectacle of so many birds in one place at one time. When a Peregrine Falcon or other predator scares a group of birds into the sky, they form a tight flock that performs precise, evasive maneuvers. This all-in-unison flight is called a murmuration.

A group of Sandpipers is a *bind, contradiction, fling,* or *time-step.*

Rufous Hummingbird
(Selasphorus rufus)
Alaska migrant

There's no mistaking the male Rufous Hummingbird, with its glittering orange throat patch and copper-colored body. The handsome hummer flies to Alaska every spring from the southern U.S. and Mexico—about four thousand miles one way.

Hummingbirds are the only birds that can fly backwards and upside down. They do this by flipping their wings over to push against the air on the downstroke and upstroke. It works very well, but takes a lot of energy. Hummers have to eat up to three times their weight in insects and nectar every day to keep going. When enough food isn't available, the little birds survive by going into "torpor" mode: their heartbeat slows and their body temperature drops to conserve energy. Rufous Hummingbirds have a reputation for being especially aggressive. Some hummingbird feeders even come with advice on how to handle Rufous bullying.

A group of Hummingbirds is a *bouquet, charm, glittering,* or *shimmer.*

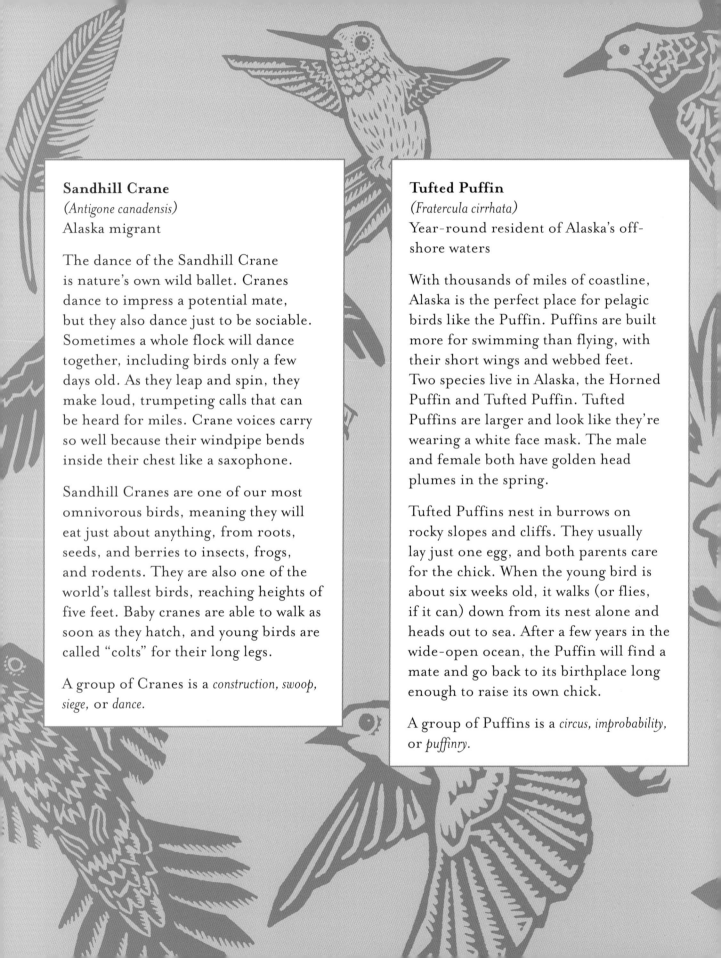

Sandhill Crane
(Antigone canadensis)
Alaska migrant

The dance of the Sandhill Crane is nature's own wild ballet. Cranes dance to impress a potential mate, but they also dance just to be sociable. Sometimes a whole flock will dance together, including birds only a few days old. As they leap and spin, they make loud, trumpeting calls that can be heard for miles. Crane voices carry so well because their windpipe bends inside their chest like a saxophone.

Sandhill Cranes are one of our most omnivorous birds, meaning they will eat just about anything, from roots, seeds, and berries to insects, frogs, and rodents. They are also one of the world's tallest birds, reaching heights of five feet. Baby cranes are able to walk as soon as they hatch, and young birds are called "colts" for their long legs.

A group of Cranes is a *construction, swoop, siege,* or *dance.*

Tufted Puffin
(Fratercula cirrhata)
Year-round resident of Alaska's off-shore waters

With thousands of miles of coastline, Alaska is the perfect place for pelagic birds like the Puffin. Puffins are built more for swimming than flying, with their short wings and webbed feet. Two species live in Alaska, the Horned Puffin and Tufted Puffin. Tufted Puffins are larger and look like they're wearing a white face mask. The male and female both have golden head plumes in the spring.

Tufted Puffins nest in burrows on rocky slopes and cliffs. They usually lay just one egg, and both parents care for the chick. When the young bird is about six weeks old, it walks (or flies, if it can) down from its nest alone and heads out to sea. After a few years in the wide-open ocean, the Puffin will find a mate and go back to its birthplace long enough to raise its own chick.

A group of Puffins is a *circus, improbability,* or *puffinry.*

Bald Eagle
(Haliaeetus leucocephalus)
Year-round Alaska resident

So much about the Bald Eagle is big! Females, which can be a third larger than males, can be three feet tall and weigh fourteen pounds. Of course such a big bird needs a big nest, and one record-setting stick nest measured nine feet across. An Eagle's eyeballs are so big that they fill most of its skull. If you could see as well as an Eagle, you would be able to spot an ant on the ground from the tenth floor of a building.

Even though they're big and powerful, Bald Eagles are known for stealing food from other birds. The scientific term for this bird piracy is "kleptoparasitism." Happily, there's more than enough food for everybody when salmon swim up Alaska's rivers to spawn. Each fall, some three thousand Bald Eagles gather along the Chilkat River for the feast—the largest gathering of Bald Eagles in the world.

A group of Eagles is a *convocation, congregation, congress,* or *aerie.*

American Dipper
(Cinclus mexicanus)
Year-round Alaska resident

This little bird is the only fully aquatic songbird in North America. Even in winter, the American Dipper plunges head-first into creeks and streams looking for insect larvae and fish eggs to eat. Beautifully adapted to a watery life, Dippers have dense feathering, waterproof oils, and nasal flaps to keep water out. They swim using their short wings, and walk underwater by gripping stones with their long toes.

Dippers stay close to their home streams year-round and almost never fly more than about nine feet above the water. They will even build their nests behind waterfalls or on boulders in the middle of a stream. The outer part of the ball-like nest is made of moss to absorb moisture and keep the grassy inner chamber dry. Dippers are one of the few birds that sing in winter, and hearing their song on a snowy day is magical.

A group of Dippers is a *ladle.*

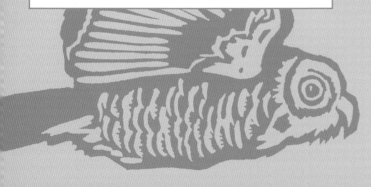

Arctic Tern
(Sterna paradisaea)
Alaska migrant

Arctic Terns fly from the top of the globe to the bottom and back again, every single year. It's the longest migration of any animal on earth. Terns can live twenty to thirty years, which means they might fly enough miles to take them to the moon and back three times!

In Alaska, Arctic Terns nest from the northern coast through the state's Southeast panhandle. The birds head south to Antarctica in midsummer, following a route over the Pacific Ocean that keeps them far offshore. Their main job up north is raising chicks. Down south it's molting, to replace worn flight feathers. Arctic Terns molt very quickly in order to be ready to fly north in early spring. By splitting their time between earth's two polar regions, Arctic Terns live in endless summertime—spending more hours in the sunshine than any other animal.

A group of Terns is a *cotillion* or *ternery*.

Great Horned Owl
(Bubo virginianus)
Year-round Alaska resident

Alaskan Great Horned Owl pairs start house hunting as early as January. They don't build their own nests, so this early timing gives them the best selection of empty, "pre-owned" nests to choose from. While they're looking for just the right spot, Owl pairs perform hooting duets that can last up to an hour. Along with hooting, they also use their ear tufts to communicate: up when the Owls are curious or alert, and down when they're aggravated.

Among the largest owls in North America, Great Horned Owls are fierce predators. Excellent hearing and eyesight help them locate prey in dim light, and special feathers let them fly silently. Great Horned Owls mostly hunt small animals like rabbits, ducks, and mice. They will cache (store) extra food in times of plenty, and if the cached food freezes, they sit on it to thaw it out.

A group of Owls is a *glaring, wisdom, parliament,* or *stare*.

Great Blue Heron
(Ardea herodias)
Year-round Alaska resident

Great Blue Herons are the picture of patience. The long-legged birds hunt by standing still in shallow water, watching and waiting. When an unwary fish or frog comes along, the Heron slowly curls back its neck and strikes quickly. Since it can't hold a fish in its feet to eat like a hawk would, the Heron swallows its prey whole.

Great Blue Herons live in both freshwater and saltwater environments. Salt and mud can be hard on feathers, but Herons have a built-in system to keep their plumage in top shape. Special sets of feathers called "powder down" grow on the bird's rump and breast. These feathers continually fray into a sort of cleaning powder that the Heron rakes through the rest of its feathers with a comblike toenail, called a "pectinate claw." Pectinate claws appear to have evolved in birds whose bills aren't very useful for preening.

A group of Great Blue Herons is called a *pose, rookery,* or *hedge.*

Common Raven
(Corvus corax)
Year-round Alaska resident

Ravens are known for their antics, so it's no wonder these smart, bold birds appear in so many traditional stories. Real-life Ravens slide down snowy roofs for fun and have been caught stealing golf balls and Easter eggs. They hang upside down from branches and telephone wires to impress each other, and find countless clever ways to show off. Ravens also seem to enjoy teasing wolves—yanking their tails and playing keep-away with sticks. Scientists believe Ravens may lead wolves to prey, which can end in plentiful leftovers for these resourceful birds.

Ravens might have the most diverse vocalizations in the animal kingdom, except for humans. Their calls range from croaks and quorks to mews, whistles, gurgles, shrieks, and knocks. They are also impressive mimics and have been heard making all kinds of sounds, from dog barks and woodpecker drumming, to dripping water and car alarms.

A group of Ravens is a *conspiracy, rant, unkindness,* or *storytelling.*

Yellow Warbler
(*Setophaga petechia*)
Alaska migrant

These little birds brighten the Alaskan landscape as they flit around in trees gleaning caterpillars and other insects from the branches. They will also dash out of the trees to catch flying bugs, a behavior called "hawking" or "sallying." Listen for Yellow Warblers in willow thickets and wetlands. Their songs are loud, clear, and... warbly! Males do all the singing, but females give short chipping calls. Young males learn songs from their fathers, and make up song variations of their own. A male Yellow Warbler might know over a dozen songs, each with a different meaning. For example, one song might be to attract a mate, while another warns away trespassers.

A popular memory cue to help identify this bird's song is: "Sweet, sweet, I'm so sweet." It's a useful pattern to listen for, but remember that Yellow Warbler songs can vary from bird to bird.

A group of Yellow Warblers is a *stream, sweetness,* or *trepidation.*

Northern Flicker
(*Colaptes auratus*)
Alaska migrant

When a Flicker hammers on something, it isn't trying to peck a hole; it just wants to make noise to communicate. The birds have distinctive calls but no songs, so drumming is used to court a mate and to defend territory. A Flicker "drumroll" lasts about a second, during which their bills can hit the surface twenty-five times. A layer of spongy bone at the base of its bill saves the bird from getting a concussion.

When a Flicker does want to peck a hole, it chisels instead of hammers. As members of the Woodpecker family, Flickers are "primary" cavity nesters. This means they chisel or dig out holes in trees that are later used by "secondary" cavity nesters like Kestrels, Tree Swallows, Pygmy Owls, and Goldeneye Ducks.

A group of Flickers is a *guttering, menorah,* or *Peterson.*

Bird Words

adaptation: evolutionary changes that help an animal survive and thrive in its environment. For example, the Ptarmigan's feathered snowshoes are an adaptation to life in the far north.

aquatic: having biological adaptations to live in or around water. Examples of aquatic adaptations include webbed feet, special eyelids, and oil glands for waterproofing.

cache: to store for future use. Great Horned Owls might cache prey animals, while Chickadees, Clark's Nutcrackers, and certain other birds may store tens of thousands of seeds in a single year.

cavity nest: a nesting chamber excavated into the trunk of a dead or dying tree

clime: the climate of a place

corvid: a bird in the Corvidae family, which includes ravens, crows, jays, and magpies

gleaning: plucking insects from surfaces like leaves, branches, or the ground

habitat: an ecosystem that provides the food, water, shelter, and space an animal needs to survive

larvae: one of the four stages that most insects have in their life cycle (egg, larva, pupa, and adult). The larvae of many familiar land insects (like dragonflies, mosquitoes, mayflies, and stoneflies) live that stage of their lives in the water.

metabolic rate: the speed at which chemical processes in the body turn food into energy to power the muscles and organs

molting: shedding old feathers so new ones can grow in. Good feather condition is important to a bird's survival. Feathers allow a bird to fly, help it attract a mate, and keep it warm, dry, and camouflaged from predators.

HURRICANE HUNTER

Paul Flaherty

TRACKING DANGEROUS STORMS

Paul Flaherty's head has been in the clouds since second grade. It all started when a Boston TV weatherman named Dick Albert visited his school. "I told him someday I was going to be a meteorologist," says Paul. That's a scientist who studies and forecasts weather.

He meant it. Every chance he could, young Paul hurried home—or to his grandparents' house nearby—to watch the local weather reports. Thunderstorms, heat waves, high winds, thick fog . . . it all fascinated him. "Whenever I saw something, I didn't just think, 'That's kind of neat,'" he says. "I thought, 'How does that happen?' That's really what I was excited about—trying to figure out how things happen and why they happen. The unpredictability of weather was partly what sparked my interest."

Growing up in New England, the budding scientist was particularly inspired by extreme weather conditions. The Blizzard of '78, which blanketed the Boston area with two to four feet of snow in less than a day and a half, "amazed" him. Years later in September 1985, Hurricane Gloria's powerful presence left a lasting impression.

"Being the weather-crazed kid that I was, I remember watching news reports about the storm quite a few days before it made landfall," says Paul. "The Weather Channel had been on the air for three years at the time, and I was always glued to it. I lived about a half-mile from the beach, so everyone wondered if we should be concerned and possibly evacuate the area, but officials deemed it safe to stay."

As Gloria crept her way up the eastern seaboard toward Massachusetts, people stocked up on supplies and prepared for the worst. "My friends and I were excited, because school was canceled for the next day in advance, which meant we had a long weekend," says Paul. "Well, it certainly became a long weekend—a weekend plus a few extra days.

The February Blizzard of '78 buried cars in several feet of snow and stranded motorists for days. It also stirred Paul Flaherty's passion for extreme weather.

"I worked at a local convenience store called PJ's Mini Mart, about two blocks from my house. My bosses—Pete and Jack—were concerned about the area losing power, so they had us make many, many bags of ice." (The ice would help people to keep food fresh if refrigerators stopped working.)

On September 27, Gloria's winds kicked up—reportedly reaching as high as 109 miles per hour in some places. "With the winds came the falling trees," says Paul. Then downed power lines. By midday, dark skies cast an ominous shadow over the area and fueled intermittent rain squalls.

"Although my parents told me not to go, one of my best friends and I headed to Wollaston Beach," says Paul. "I couldn't believe how much stronger the wind was blowing there," he says. "The sand blinded me at times, and it was the first time I saw the ocean crash over the seawall."

What Paul recalls most vividly, however, is the mesmerizing sky. "I was always looking at the clouds," he says, "but I had never seen clouds moving so fast! It was like watching cars go by on the highway . . . When I saw those clouds that day, it was no longer that I wanted to know more about the weather but that I *had* to know more about the weather. At that point, there was no turning back: while meteorology remained my

Paul's interest in meteorology was sparked by a school visit from a Boston TV weatherman. Today, he inspires students—including middle-schooler Michael Morley.

Legendary Daredevils: The first people to fly into the eye of a hurricane did it on a dare. In 1943, U.S. Air Force pilot Joseph Duckworth and navigator Ralph O'Hair took to the stormy skies—without telling anyone—to prove that their single-engine plane could withstand any weather. The pair successfully completed their mission and paved the way for others—including the 53rd Weather Reconnaissance Squadron, now based in Biloxi, Mississippi. These hurricane hunters survey storms in the Atlantic, Caribbean, Gulf of Mexico, and Central Pacific for the National Hurricane Center and have been flying more than sixty years.

interest, tropical storms became my passion. I didn't know then that people could fly into hurricanes."

STORM SCIENCE

As planned, Paul studied meteorology in college, where he learned about the atmosphere, weather patterns, and climate changes. He worked in a special security unit of the United States Air Force and eventually went on to teach meteorology to military students. One day he spotted a job posting for a hurricane hunter and thought, *Wouldn't it be* amazing *to fly inside a hurricane?*

Today, that's exactly what Paul does for a living—flies into the eye of some of the world's most destructive storms, gathering information about their strength and direction to help keep people safe. The data he collects helps weather forecasters track the path of potentially deadly storms and alert communities through television, radio, and the Internet.

Hurricanes are extreme tropical cyclones—spiraling storms that form over warm seas and rotate counterclockwise. Fueled by heat and moisture, hurricanes pack winds of 74 miles per hour or more, with gusts that can top 200 miles. While each storm varies greatly in size and intensity, hurricanes typically extend more than 300 miles wide and move at 10 to 20 miles per hour. On average, they survive about nine days.

Hurricane hunters—including pilots, navigators, and meteorologists—carefully plan each mission before taking to the air.

Hurricanes that occur west of the International Date Line in the Pacific Ocean are called typhoons, while those that take place in the Indian Ocean are called cyclones.

This satellite image of Hurricane Katrina was taken in the early afternoon on August 28, 2005, by NASA's Terra satellite. At landfall, Katrina's winds topped 125 miles per hour.

A cross section of a hurricane reveals its three primary parts: the eye, or relatively calm center that's typically ten to forty miles long; the eye wall, a towering mass of storm clouds surrounding the eye column that produce violent winds and rains; and rain bands, curved stretches of thunderstorms projecting from the eye that sometimes spawn tornadoes. Moving from the outer edge of a hurricane to its center, you'd first encounter light rain and wind, and then a dry and weak breeze, reverting back to increasingly heavier rain and stronger wind—over and over again—with each period of rainfall and wind becoming longer and more intense toward the eye, say officials at the National Weather Service.

Hurricane hunters such as Paul, who works for the National Oceanic and Atmospheric Administration (NOAA), fly straight through these storm layers into a hurricane's eye. As meteorologist and flight director, Paul leads the crew into the center of a hurricane and determines the safest way to snake through the blinding winds and rains of the eye wall.

How can planes fly in such high winds?

"The plane doesn't always stay so steady," says Paul. But it's not the high winds that cause the problems; it's the wind shear, either vertical or horizontal. Wind shear happens when there's a sudden change in wind speed or direction along a plane's flight path. "So if we fly in a very strong storm but the winds don't increase or decrease rapidly throughout the eye wall, we will have relatively little horizontal shear and it should be a smoother ride." However, when storms have "hot spots" of strong vertical shear—powerful air currents called updrafts and downdrafts—"then the ride could become quite rough." Developing storms usually have the most dangerous drafts, says Paul. "It's my job to keep us out of these areas as best as I can."

To do this, Paul relies on radar equipment and analytical skills gained through years of experience. "I have to keep in mind that the storm is moving and spinning," he says. "So what's directly in front of me on radar, or what's directly in front of the aircraft at the time we're getting close to the storm, may not be what's still in front of me by the time we get there."

NOAA flies two four-engine WP-3D Orion turboprop planes directly into a hurricane's eye. A turboprop engine allows for a near instantaneous response when pilots need to accelerate or decelerate, explains Paul. This is *extremely important* when entering hurricane eye-wall conditions. Turboprop engines are also better equipped to handle a hurricane's powerful precipitation than the typical turbojet engine found in commercial airliners. They're especially designed to limit the amount of water entering the engine, says Paul.

The "P-3" planes—one affectionately nicknamed Kermit the Frog and the other Miss Piggy—feature three types of radar. The

ABOVE: Curved stretches of thunderstorms, called rain bands, project out from the eye of a hurricane. The closer to the eye, the more violent the storms. Note the red areas in the image above, which indicate bands of heavy rain. BELOW: Hurricane hunters for NOAA carve through the eye wall of a hurricane flying in Lockheed WP-3D Orion turboprop planes. The P-3s, which carry a crew of eighteen to twenty people and cruise at 345 miles per hour, allow scientists to collect storm data at altitudes of 1,500 to 25,000 feet. The information helps forecasters track and predict a hurricane's intensity and movements.

Hurricane hunters fly straight through storm layers into the eye of a hurricane. When inside the eye, they're surrounded by a wall of clouds that stretches thousands of feet high and tilts backwards—creating a stadium effect. Above them are blue skies and below, stormy seas.

first is a "typical nose radar. But this only lets you see what's happening in front of you," explains Paul. The second is a special fuselage or "belly" radar that provides a 360-degree horizontal view around the airplane with every "sweep."

"When we're inside the hurricane, I'm able to see not only what's happening in front of us, but what is happening in every direction," says Paul. "This lets me keep an eye on the entire storm at all times, even when it's behind us. Sometimes in a rough storm, the safest way out might be off to the side, or even the way we came in. The belly radar allows me to keep that in mind."

A third type of radar, called a Doppler radar, sits in the plane's tail. Like the belly radar, it sweeps 360 degrees, only vertically. "As we go into a hurricane," says Paul, "the tail radar will let me see the heights of the eye wall, as well as where some of the strongest updrafts may be located. If we are flying through lines of thunderstorms or along a rain band, the tail will give me a lot of great meteorological data. But in the eye of a hurricane, or when approaching the storm, it's the belly radar, primarily, and the nose radar that I'm glued to."

Unlike the P-3 turboprop plane, NOAA's sleek and technically sophisticated Gulfstream-IV jet (shown in front) flies around developing hurricanes instead of through them. Cruising at 530 miles per hour, the G-4 collects data from every level from 45,000 feet down to provide forecasters with a three-dimensional view of steering currents. This information supplements the data collected by the P-3s.

When they're not in the air, hurricane hunter planes are maintained and operated out of NOAA's Aircraft Operations Center at MacDill Air Force Base in Tampa, Florida.

INTO THE EYE

When the time comes to carve through a hurricane's eye wall, the Fasten Seat Belt light flashes red and the crew prepares for a bumpy ride into the center of the storm. The team—consisting of pilots, navigators, researchers, technicians, and reporters—buckles in and checks for loose items. The potential to get hit pretty hard going in is always there, Paul says. "So we look around and make sure everything is strapped down, and then we hold on and just wait."

After a choppy ride drilling through wind, rain, and turbulence, the plane reaches the hurricane's center. Suddenly, all is calm. In the eye, you are surrounded by a 30,000- to 50,000-foot wall of clouds that tilts backwards and creates a stadium effect, says Paul. "When you look up, you see clear blue skies." If the sun happens to be rising at the time, the views can be spectacular. No time for sightseeing, however. The team's on a mission.

Their goal? To find the "absolute center" of the hurricane and mark it for the National Hurricane Center. The eye is critical to understanding the storm's central air pressure and how it is changing, explains Paul. Air pressure is the weight of the atmosphere—the blanket of air surrounding the earth—pressing down on objects. If the central air pressure drops inside the column of a hurricane's eye, that tells meteorologists that wind speeds will most likely increase, says Paul. "If the pressure rises, winds are expected to weaken."

One way hurricane hunters measure air pressure is by launching a small device called a Global Positioning System (GPS) dropwindsonde from the back of the plane.

Storm Post: During missions, Paul Flaherty operates from the flight director's station in the P-3 (behind the cockpit). The station is equipped with radar displays, two satellite phones, a laptop computer, and various sensors—including one that tells Paul how much water is in the clouds the plane flies through.

As the "sonde" floats down through the eye wall and into the sea, it collects data such as pressure, temperature, humidity, wind speed, and wind direction. This information is radioed back to the plane at two Hertz, or twice per second, so meteorologists such as Paul can analyze the data and send it via satellite to the Hurricane Center, as well as to the National Center for Environment Prediction. There, forecasters feed the information into computer models that simulate likely scenarios and allow them to track hurricanes and look for trends: Is the storm losing strength or growing stronger? Has it peaked? When and where will it land?

To provide the most accurate answers, hurricane hunters generally fly through storms several times during their nine-to-ten-hour missions. Flying patterns such as the "figure 4" allows the crew to sample four quadrants of a storm—for example, north, south, east, and west—and "hit the center of the eye twice." In general, forecasters prefer that hurricane hunters make two figure 4s through a storm. "In some cases, we have flown into the eye many more times," says Paul. "With Hurricane Jeanne [September 2004], for example, I flew into the eye twenty-six times over three days."

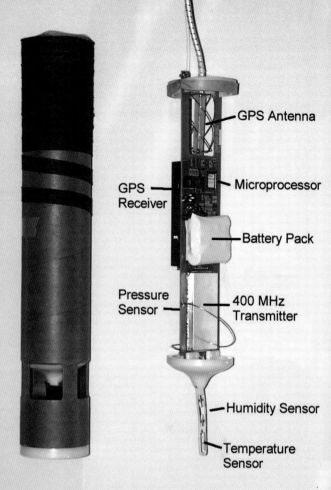

GPS Antenna
GPS Receiver
Microprocessor
Battery Pack
Pressure Sensor
400 MHz Transmitter
Humidity Sensor
Temperature Sensor

ABOVE: Close-up of a dropwindsonde.

RISKY BUSINESS

While Paul spends much of his time flying through storms during hurricane season, he doesn't consider himself a thrill-seeker. "People think that you must be an adrenaline junkie to do this," he says. "But I just have a passion for

LEFT: Ready to Roll: Electronics technician Chuck Rasco shows how he prepares to launch a GPS dropwindsonde from a chute in the back of a P-3 turboprop plane. The device, which is released in the center of a hurricane's eye, floats down to the sea on a small parachute and collects information such as air pressure and wind speed. Twelve to twenty-four sondes—each costing about six hundred dollars—are dropped during a flight's mission.

Visual Aid: One of the highlights of the meterologist flight director's station on the P-3 aircraft is a bubble window, such as the one shown, which allows Paul to stick his head outside and look forward, above, and around the plane. "Visual observations are a big part of my job," he says.

the weather. While we're all aware that there's a bit of danger to the job, we try to surround ourselves with the best people. We work as a team to cover each other and to keep it as safe as possible."

In 2003, for example, Paul's plane lost the use of one of its engines while flying through Hurricane Isabel. "The crew did exactly what it was supposed to do to get us back safely," he says. "When something like this happens, we immediately terminate the science mission and head back to base, because flying on three engines instead of four puts more stress on those other engines." The team was lucky that the engine failed just as the plane was heading back toward the storm. "It would have been a lot scarier if we had been inside the eye when it happened, because then we'd have had to find our way out through the eye wall with only three engines—something we really wouldn't want to do."

Others haven't been so fortunate. Jeff Masters, NOAA's flight meteorologist on a mission heading for Hurricane Hugo's eye in September 1989 describes the chilling scene.

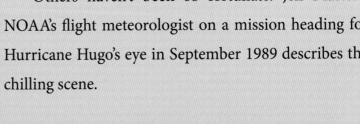

HUNTING HUGO: DISASTER

"*Thick dark clouds suddenly envelop the aircraft. A*

titanic fist of wind, three times the force of gravity, smashes us. I am thrown into the computer console, bounce off, and for one terrifying instant find myself looking DOWN at a precipitous angle at Sean [the navigator] across the aisle from me.

"A second massive jolt rocks the aircraft. Gear loosened by the previous turbulence flies about the inside of the aircraft, bouncing off walls, ceiling, and crew members . . . Our 200-pound life raft breaks loose and hurtles into the ceiling . . .

"A third terrific blow, almost six times the force of gravity, staggers the airplane. Clip boards, flight bags, and headsets sail past my head as I am hurled into the console. Terrible thundering crashing sounds boom through the cabin; I hear crew members crying out. I scream inwardly. 'This is what it feels like to die in battle . . .'"

"The aircraft lurches out of control into a hard right bank. We plunge toward the ocean, our number three engine in flames. Debris hangs from the number four engine.

"The turbulence suddenly stops. The clouds part. The darkness lifts. We fall into the eye of Hurricane Hugo . . .

"For several eternal terrifying seconds, I watch the massive, white-frothed waves below us grow huge and close. I wait for impact, praying for survival. With two engines damaged, both on the same wing, I know that our odds are not good."

The Hurricane Hugo crew miraculously made it out alive that day as pilots pulled the plane out of the dive "a perilous 880 feet from the water." But their fate easily could have gone the way of a handful of other hurricane-hunting specialists who lost their lives flying severe storms.

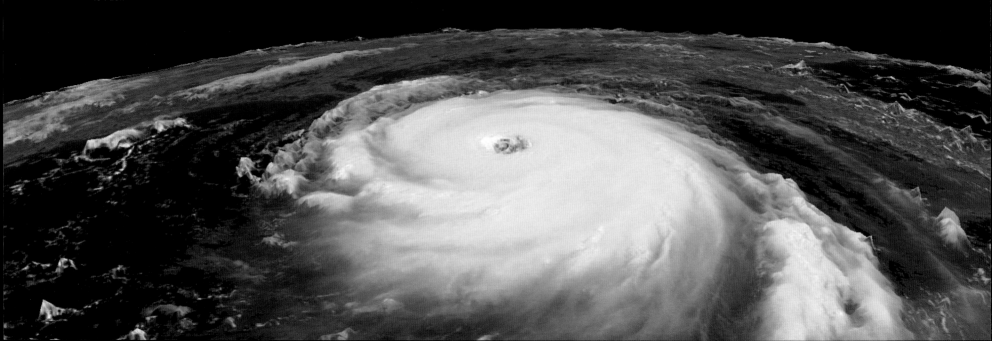

UPPER LEFT: Forecasters correctly predicted Hurricane Katrina's path with the help of data collected by hurricane hunters.

BELOW: A satellite image of Katrina from about 22,000 miles above the equator.

RIGHT: A sampling of Katrina's devastation. The damaged home belongs to Paul.

Despite such dangers, the rewards of hurricane hunting far outweigh the risks, says Paul. Hurricane Katrina's devastating effects on the Gulf Coast states of Louisiana, Mississippi, and Alabama in 2005 made that especially clear. "I flew Katrina for five nights starting when it was a tropical storm off Miami," he says. "I sat there and watched as it got closer and closer to the coastal areas where I used to live in Biloxi, Mississippi. When I saw where it had made landfall, I just couldn't believe it."

The day after Katrina struck, Paul surveyed the area. He was "in shock" during the entire damage-assessment flight. "So many of the restaurants that I used to go to were no longer physically there . . . the beach had taken over. So many people that I used to work with and all my friends from the

neighborhood where I lived lost everything. The house I built had taken on fourteen feet of water."

Still, Paul's friends and neighbors were grateful to escape Katrina's wrath with their lives. Advance warning systems and data gathered directly from the eye of the storm helped save them and the hundreds of thousands of people who evacuated the area early.

"A big part of the reason [people survived] is because we were out there flying in the storm, doing our job," says Paul. "We were told by the National Hurricane Center that if you run the [computer] models and remove the data we collected in Hurricane Katrina, the landfall forecast is off by two hundred miles. The loss of life most likely would have been many times worse. That really put an exclamation point for me on why we do what we do and is the primary reason why I'll be ready to go back out there each and every season."

QUICK QUESTIONS
HURRICANE HUNTER

Q. Who flies on hurricane hunter missions?

A. We generally have two pilots and a flight engineer up front on the P-3 hurricane hunter turboprop planes. Right behind them sits the flight director/meteorologist and the navigator. We also have a minimum of three technicians in the back to keep everything running. If anything goes wrong at my station, I call for them.

Q. Does anyone else ever fly with you?

A. Yes. We're involved in a variety of worldwide meteorological, oceanographic, and environmental studies, so quite often we'll have scientists on board such as chemists who want to sample the air. We fly with a lot of weather instruments in development for research projects. Many times, these instruments come from universities, and we'll have the students and professors who are working on them fly with us. During hurricane season, we also have quite a bit of TV, newspaper, and radio crews fly along.

Q. What do you eat on a hurricane-hunting mission?

A. Everyone usually brings a bag lunch. Most people bring food from the local sub shop. But some bring foods to help settle their stomachs, since we sometimes get bounced around a bit. They might bring a stack of crackers and bread and chew on that the whole flight. Others get a little crazy and may bring along bowls of chili. That's usually the last thing people want to see in the middle of a flight.

Q. Have storms become stronger and more unpredictable in recent years?

A. The question is being heavily researched, studied, and debated. If you asked me in December 2005—after the crazy 2004 and 2005 hurricane seasons—my immediate response may have been yes. But as we know, the 2006 and 2007 seasons were relatively mild. At times, it seems a change is happening. And we hear so much about it, we almost think, *It must be true*. But as scientists, we have to look at all the data before reaching a conclusion.

Q. Hurricane season runs from June 1 to November 30. What do you do when the season ends?

A. Most people don't realize we fly year-round. Last year, we flew air-pollution studies for six weeks in Houston, Texas. We also had people in St. John's, Newfoundland, who flew storms in the North Atlantic Ocean to help calibrate (adjust) satellites that estimate wind speed. I've also flown out of Costa Rica, where we worked to better understand how tropical storms are formed. In addition, we've flown out of Ireland, Hawaii, and Alaska, where our goal was to improve winter storm forecasting. A few years ago we traveled to southern Illinois to fly severe Midwest storms so forecasters can better predict what triggers them. Called bow echo storms because of their bow-shape appearance on radar displays, these storms can generate tornadoes, flash floods, hurricane-force winds, and massive amounts of lightning. In fact, on my last flight of that mission, we were struck by lightning thirty-four times!

The P-3 planes boast a proud history of service, with a symbol for each hurricane pierced highlighted on its side. Among the more famous hurricanes this plane has flown through are hurricanes Andrew (1992), Katrina (2005), and Felix (2007).

CAVE
WOMAN
Hazel Barton
MINING MICROBES

Nichol Creek Cave winds seven miles beneath a sleepy Kentucky mountain. Lush foliage and a fifty-foot rock cliff camouflage its secret, watery entrance. Looking to explore the cave's inner beauty and biology is British-born Hazel Barton, a microbiologist at Northern Kentucky University. Hazel hunts the earth's hidden frontiers—from glacial ice caves in Greenland to underwater caves deep in the jungles of Mexico—for some of its tiniest inhabitants. These single-cell organisms, called microbes, include bacteria and fungi. They live everywhere—from in the air we breathe to inside our bodies—and are considered the oldest form of life on earth.

Some hardy microbes thrive in places never before thought possible, such as searing-hot ocean springs and the bottom of bitter-cold Antarctic lakes. Scientists refer to these super-resilient creatures as "extremophiles." They believe the microbes' ability to flourish under extreme conditions may provide insights to everything from life on Mars to cleaning the environment. Hazel Barton studies extremophiles that

Hazel rappels down a drop in the Pandora's Boxwork area of Black Chasm Cavern, Amador County, California. The cave is noted for its helictites—cave formations that grow as small twisted structures projecting at different angles.

Microbes, such as the bacteria pictured in the background, live everywhere—in the air and in our bodies. Microbes that live in extremely hot, cold, acidic, or starved conditions are called extremophiles.

Among the life forms found atop redwoods are lichens—unique organisms resulting from a symbiotic relationship between a fungus and algae. The lichen pictured, named *Cetraria chlorophylla,* thrives in sunny areas. Steve found this one growing on a redwood branch 355 feet above the ground.

out of the soil accumulations in the tops of redwood trees," says Steve. "We found oak trees and laurel trees . . . woody plants that live up in the crowns of these enormous ancient redwoods. They never get very big—these trees on trees—but the fact they exist and can live for decades is amazing."

Plants and animals thrive on redwoods in part because the trees reiterate—or repeat themselves—at their crown, sprouting new trunks and branches that can support hundreds of pounds of rich canopy soils. (These soils, made of decomposed leaves and debris, accumulate at the base of new redwood trunks over time.) "When a tree's main trunk is damaged, and the leader [the highest shoot] is killed for one reason or another, it has one of two options," explains Steve. The tree can replace it with a single reiterated trunk that would continue growing and result in "a bend or kink where the break and recovery occurred." Or it could replace the leader with multiple trunks, which often happens when the damage is more severe or occurs later in the tree's life. "These reiterated trunks grow like the trees do when they're young, with a vertical main stem and horizontal branches" that fan up and outward, he says. "In some really impressive trees, dozens and dozens of reiterated trunks form a whole dome-shaped upper crown of the tree . . . creating a candelabra effect."

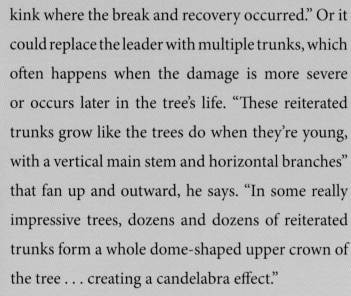

Rich canopy soils accumulate in redwoods over time, allowing plants such as this fern to thrive. The soils, which are made of decomposed foliage and debris, vary in amounts from tree to tree, but some redwoods hold hundreds and hundreds of pounds. These soil mats in the junctures of limbs and trunks act as sponges, catching rain and keeping areas moist for plants and animals.

Old-growth redwoods often reiterate—or repeat themselves—after they've been damaged. New trunks and branches sprout and fan up and outward like the original tree.

CANOPY CLIMB

It's a long way up into a redwood—and the first step's the most dangerous. "Redwoods are the tallest trees in the world, but they have a very particular kind of structure when they grow in forests," says Steve, a professor at Humboldt State University in Arcata, California. "The big trees don't have branches down low to the ground." Often the trunk's bare for hundreds of feet, with the first sturdy boughs emerging as high up as twenty-five stories.

To gain a solid footing and begin his climb, Steve fires a bolt from a high-powered crossbow over the tree's branches and launches a fishing line that's tied to it. The bolt then drags the fishing line back to the ground, and this is used to haul a rope up, over, and down. After carefully rigging the tree, Steve "jugs" up the redwood's trunk to the crown's base—all the while suspended from a harness so he can tread lightly and avoid injuring the tree's bark.

Going Up: Once a tree is carefully rigged, a climber jugs up its trunk to the base of the crown.

"When you first ascend a tree, you're not quite sure what you've shot your line over," he says. Dead branches can dislodge and fall. So initially, getting to the crown can be risky. "Once you're up in the top, you can reestablish your climbing path through the crown so that you can avoid any hazards that might exist. And these large redwood trees have lots of hazards, because they've been battered by storms over the centuries." Many trees are more than a thousand years old and may have huge, unstable chunks of deadwood—nicknamed widow-makers—that can break loose, Steve says. "You just have to be careful and avoid those places so that they don't fall off on you or anybody on the ground."

Once while climbing a tall redwood, Steve nearly died.

"After shooting my line into the tree with a bow, I ascended the rope," he

After the first climber reaches the crown of this giant sequoia, two others ascend and measure the main trunk's diameter at regular intervals. Whereas the coast redwood is the world's tallest tree, the giant sequoia is the world's most massive tree.

recounts. "When I reached about forty meters above the ground, there was a loud snapping sound and I began to fall." Incidents like these often happen during a first ascent, so at first he wasn't too alarmed. "However," he says, "after falling ten meters, I panicked and let out a scream of terror. Suddenly, at thirty meters above the ground, my fall stopped and I was jerked to a halt on the rope—spinning in space . . .with the sound of my scream ringing in my ears."

As his heart pounded, Steve courageously continued his climb until at seventy meters he reached the limb that had saved his life. "Apparently," he says, "five meters above the limb, my line had passed over a broken branch. When the branch fell, my rope pinned it to the top of the sturdy limb below. Had the branch not become trapped on the limb, the fall surely would have killed me."

EXTREME EXPLORATIONS

Some redwood journeys last a day, as the scientist stealthfully moves about the branches and "skywalks," or explores a tree's crown while dangling in midair and without touching it. Other missions last longer and require stays in high-rise hammocks called tree boats. Every tree is structurally unique, says Steve—especially in the old-growth forest. "The trees are hundreds and hundreds of years old, and they've got so much character because they've been hammered by lightning and fire and wind and falling neighbors. And they've responded to all these injuries over time."

Many old redwoods, for instance, have survived fires through the centuries, says

Fire caves are dark, shady places. Still, some plants manage to spring to life in them, such as this huckleberry bush.

Steve. "Parts of their crown will burn and if the burn gets into a pocket of decay or where a big limb has fallen off, it can often hollow out a chamber." These chambers—or fire caves—can grow with each new fire, and over a tree's lifetime it may form several, he says. Fire caves are dark, shady places, so few plants grow in them. "Occasionally there will be a shrub, like a huckleberry bush, that's rooted in the cave, but its branches extend out of the mouth of the cave . . . A lot of times you'll see flying squirrel nests in the cave, or you'll see raccoon, owl, or ravens' nests."

MEASURING UP

One important facet of Steve's work involves mapping redwoods to learn more about their structure and how they grow. Despite years of forest research, we still have a great deal to learn about the inner workings of individual trees, says Steve. How does a redwood respond to weather changes and conditions such as droughts? How does the tree use water that it drinks from the soil and absorbs from rain and fog? To help unravel the riddles of a redwood, he and a team of climbers measure a tree by stretching a tape around its main trunk, limbs, branches, and any reiterated trunks they may find. "We map their diameters at different heights through the crown, and then chart their XYZ coordinates [numbers representing a position point] so they can be built in three dimensions on a computer," says Steve. "That computer model can be used to calculate things like wood volume, bark surface, and leaf biomass [the total weight of the leaves]."

If you're studying a radish, it's easy to weigh it or calculate how many leaves it has, notes Steve. "But when you're studying a redwood, how do you know how big it is?" Mapping is a critical step to understanding a tree's dimensions. "Until we know precisely how many leaves a tree has, how much surface area it has, how much wood it has, and how the different branches are sized and distributed in the crown, we're really never going to be able to understand how the tree grows, let alone how much it grows."

Some redwoods spindle toward the sky at surprising heights. In 2006, naturalists Chris Atkins and Michael Taylor discovered a towering titan in a remote valley of

An important part of Steve Sillett's work involves mapping trees to learn more about their structure and how they grow. Here he notes the diameter of a reiterated trunk measured by his colleague Cameron Williams.

Steve measures the amount of light available to the leaves in the crown of this redwood that's more than 370 feet tall by using a digital camera on a self-leveling mount.

56

California's Redwood National Park. The two believed it to be the world's tallest living tree. To verify their find, Steve measured the redwood: first by beaming a laser to calculate the tree's height from the ground, and then—the most accurate way—by climbing the redwood and dropping a weighted fiberglass tape from the top.

The result? A record-breaking 379.1 feet. "We were blown away," says Steve, who wants to protect the tree by keeping its location secret. "That tree was four feet taller than the champ before it." Steve expects the soaring redwood to enjoy a long reign as top tree. "I really have a hard time imagining that we're going to dethrone it anytime soon," he says. "I think it will slowly keep growing, an inch or two a year . . . then there might be a drought and its top will die back, and another tree—probably the previous record-

Steve measures the crown of this giant sequoia using ropes and tools that allow him to move much like Spider-Man.

Sensors mounted in trees collect information for scientists, including measurements of light, wind, temperature, humidity, and precipitation. By monitoring the physical conditions around a redwood, called the microclimate, scientists can gain a better understanding of how a tree's environment affects its growth. Here Steve clears debris from a rain gauge.

In September 2006, Steve Sillett climbed, measured, and confirmed the world's tallest living tree at a record-breaking 379.1 feet. Here's a view of its top. "The only evident damage was from a woodpecker," says Steve.

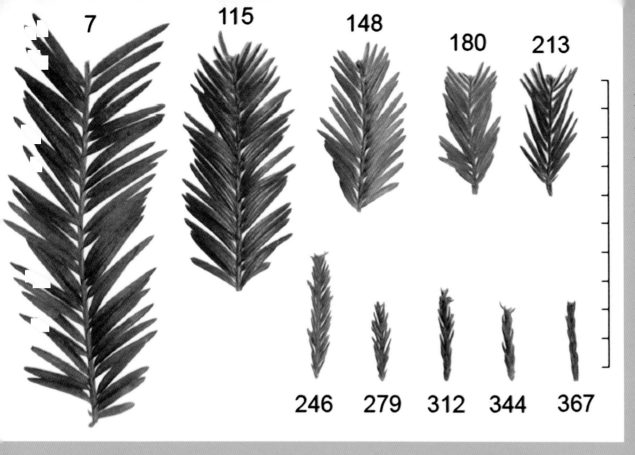

7 **115** **148** **180** **213**

246 **279** **312** **344** **367**

Changes at the Top: A redwood's leaves tend to be smaller and scalier higher up in the tree. That's because less water makes it to the upper branches, so redwood leaves become progressively less expanded with increasing height. This shortage of water also ultimately limits how tall the tree can grow. Numbers represent height above the ground in feet.

holder at 375.3 feet—will become the new tallest tree. But we'll see . . . We're keeping track of all the tallest trees. This is important in the face of climate change, pollution, and logging. Right now we have one hundred and fifty trees taller than three hundred and fifty feet, and they're all redwood."

Theoretically, the tallest tree and its counterparts could grow more than 410 feet tall, estimates Steve, who has teamed with several colleagues to study the limits to tree height. After examining many factors, the researchers found that what generally stops redwoods from reaching their maximum potential heights—besides fires, wind, and lightning—is water stress. Redwoods are thirsty trees, says Steve. The tallest grow along streams, in moist, rich soils, and drink hundreds of gallons of water a day. Rain and fog provide some moisture, which is absorbed through the needlelike leaves, he explains. But most of the water trees use to grow comes from their roots—and that water's pulled up all the way through the wood against gravity.

Imagine the water in a redwood flowing inside pipes that connect from the roots and soil to the rest of the tree. As water evaporates from the tree's leaves through tiny pores called stomata, it pulls up more water behind it—slowly but surely moving moisture to the upper crown. But the higher the water has to travel up a tree, the more difficult it becomes to resist the forces of gravity. This can lead to air entering the pipeline and blocking the flow of water, explains Steve. "If this happens a lot, then the top of the tree can't get enough water and may die back." One way a tree works to prevent water loss is to close its stomata. However, since stomata also let carbon dioxide into the leaves, this limits photosynthesis—the chemical process by which the plant produces sugar (food) from carbon dioxide, water, and sunlight.

A redwood's leaves also tend to be smaller and scalier as you move up the tree, says Steve. "All these changes in leaves as a tree grows taller may combine to slow, and eventually stop, its height growth."

BRANCHING OUT

Studying how redwoods grow is one way scientists such as Steve are deepening our understanding of the earth's tallest trees, which, in recent years, have been dying or showing signs of severe stress. Scientists are assessing the problem and working to find solutions to improve the situation now and for the future. "We're starting to get a real handle on how to gather information at the whole-tree level . . . and to quantify the entire tree," he says. "Once we can do this for a large number of trees—several different species—then we're going to be able to ask some really important questions."

Among those questions: How will climate changes from pollution and global warming affect redwoods and other tall trees? Are the giants versatile enough to withstand the changes? What can people do to reduce the impacts? "I'm concerned

that we don't allow the climate to change so much that the redwood forests decline further," says Steve. "If we lose the tallest trees, future generations won't be able to marvel at the beauty of redwood forests and be truly inspired by the natural world."

For the pioneering professor, such issues propel him personally and professionally.

"You spend hours and hours measuring items in a tree," he says. "You start to learn about the tree—and each tree has its own feel. As you move around through the canopy over time, you see changes that happen to individual trees: 'There's a branch that broke off.' Or, 'Wow, that thing's really grown.' You can actually see changes from year to year in these trees, so it's always interesting to get back into an old friendly tree and see how it has changed and grown . . . It's become such a passion to do scientific work in the forest canopy. If I go without tree climbing for a few weeks, I definitely crave it."

Climbing redwoods takes courage, training, and proper equipment to stay safe. While the work is rewarding and the views are spectacular, if a climber makes one wrong move it could mean his or her life.

QUICK QUESTIONS
SKYWALKER

Q. How long is your typical redwood climb?

A. It varies from mission to mission. Sometimes we stay aloft for several days and sleep in little hammocks called tree boats. Other times, we just climb all day and come down toward sunset and return the next day.

Q. What's it like to watch the sunrise from the top of a redwood?

A. Pretty amazing. You often wake before dawn, because you can hear the birds chirping . . . It's always a little disorienting when you wake up and realize that you are waking up at the top of a redwood.* It kind of heightens your experience. You can peer over the edge of your hammock and look across the tops of the trees into the distance and watch the mist roll in. As the sun rises, there's a breathtaking view of the forest.

*Note: Climbers tie themselves to the trees to keep from rolling out of their hammocks.

Q. Do you think about the danger when you're climbing?

A. When I'm climbing to the top of a tall redwood, I'm keenly aware that the ground is hundreds of feet below me. There's a sense that if you make a mistake, you're going to kill yourself. It's very dangerous to climb trees without proper training and without good equipment. I change my main climbing ropes every year. So, yes, there's a sense of risk involved, but you minimize the risks with

Bull Creek in Humboldt Redwoods State Park is home to the world's tallest forest, with more than 100 of the 147 known redwoods taller than 350 feet, notes Steve. Almost every tree in this photo is more than 300 feet tall. "We owe a great debt of gratitude to the Save-the-Redwoods League for helping protect some fine examples of old-growth redwood forest. These forests were nearly destroyed, but there's still a chance to understand them and use this knowledge to restore some of our cut-over [previously logged] landscapes."

proper training—which takes months of time, patience, and expert instruction.*

*Note: Steve and his colleagues use an adapted version of tree-climbing techniques that have been developed by arborists, tree surgeons who work with damaged trees.

Q. How do you avoid hurting a tree when you're in it?

A. Trees are more fragile than people realize. If you run a rope over a branch and hang your weight on it, when you pull the rope back and forth, it literally saws into the bark and can damage the living tissues beneath it—including the inner bark and cambium [the thin layer of cells just beneath the bark]. Your feet also can knock off whole branches along with any ferns, mosses, lichens, and salamanders living there. Soils that build up can be trampled and greatly affected by human traffic, as well. So we always suspend ourselves above the tree surfaces using ropes connected with cambium-savers. We wrap this device around the branch and then run our climbing rope through a pulley on the bottom. This way our ropes do minimal damage to fragile habitats as we move through the canopy. We also never use spikes on our boots, because they can injure the tree with every step.

Q. Have you had any close calls due to weather?

A. We climb giant sequoias in the Sierra Nevadas (a California mountain range) during the summer, and we've had to retreat hastily out of some trees in lightning storms. That's scary. In the coast redwoods, I once neglected to check the satellite imagery and went to the top of a tall tree in January, and a gale-force winter storm came in suddenly. I was caught at the top in driving hail and freezing rain, so I had to retreat. It was miserable.

Q. You climb all types of tall trees. How is climbing an Australian eucalyptus tree different from climbing a California redwood?

A. The only thing that's similar is their height. The Australian species that I study—*Eucalyptus regnans,* also known as mountain ash and swamp gum—sheds its bark every year, so the inner layers are still green. When they're wet, they glow green. And they're slippery, and sketchy, and really weird. They're big, old, windy, nightmarish trees . . . When you get to the top, you can always see the ground. There's never a moment when you can just kind of chill. It's probably the most intimidating tree climbing. At the same time, these trees form one of the most beautiful forests I have ever seen. The canopy is full of life, including raucous cockatoos, gliding possums, and many other amazing animals.

One of the most intimidating tall trees to climb is *Eucalyptus regnans* in Australia, says Steve. It's a flowering tree without a thick leafy crown, "so you can always see the ground." Pictured climbing is Steve's wife, Marie Antoine, who also is a botanist and studies forest canopies. Farther below are their colleagues Jim Spickler (yellow helmet) and Bob Van Pelt (red helmet).

WANT TO DIG DEEPER?

PUBLICATIONS

• *Cave Sleuths* (Science on the Edge series) by Laurie Lindop (Twenty-first Century Books, 2006).

• *Coast Redwood: A Natural and Cultural History* edited by John Evarts and Marjorie Popper (Cachuma Press, 2001).

• *Exploring Caves: Journeys into the Earth* by Nancy Holler Aulenbach and Hazel A. Barton with Marfe Ferguson Delano (National Geographic Society, 2001).

• *Hurricane & Tornado* (DK Eyewitness Books) by Jack Challoner (DK Publishing, 2004).

• *Hurricane Force: In the Path of America's Deadliest Storms* (New York Times) by Joseph B. Treaster (Kingfisher, 2007).

• *Taking Science to the Extreme* (Discovery Channel Young Scientist Challenge) by Rosanna Hansen and Sherry Gerstein (Jossey-Bass, 2006).

• *A Voice for the Redwoods* by Loretta Halter and illustrated by Emily du Houx (Polar Bear & Company, 2002).

DVDS

• *Adventures in Wild California* (IMAX). MMI Image Entertainment, 2001.

• *Hurricane Katrina: The Storm That Drowned a City* (NOVA). WGBH (Boston), 2006.

• *Journey into Amazing Caves.* MacGillivray Freeman Films, 2001.

WEBSITES

• Cyberflight into the Eye of a Hurricane: www.hurricanehunters.com/cyberflight.html

• Hazel Barton's Cave Science: www.cavescience.com

• Hunting Hugo—meteorologist Jeff Master's chilling story: www.wunderground.com/education/hugo1.asp

• Journey into Amazing Caves: www.amazingcaves.com

• Mammoth Cave—National Park Service: www.nps.gov/maca

• Microbe World: www.microbeworld.org/microbes

• National Hurricane Center: www.nhc.noaa.gov

• National Oceanic and Atmospheric Administration: www.noaa.gov

• Redwood National and State Parks: www.nps.gov/redw

• Save the Redwoods League: www.savetheredwoods.org

• Steve Sillett's Redwood Forest Ecology site: www.humboldt.edu/~sillett

Fourteen-year-old Aeron Horton of Ohio inspects a helictite. He and his parents spend many weekends underground, exploring and mapping new territory.

NOAA flies two hurricane-hunting P-3 planes directly into the eye of hurricanes. One plane is nicknamed Kermit the Frog and the other Miss Piggy.

HURRICANE HUNTER

Air pressure: the weight of the atmosphere pressing down on objects. Generally, high pressure (dense, heavy air) is associated with good weather and low pressure (lighter air) is associated with bad weather.

Atmosphere: the mixture of gases between the earth and space.

Barometer: a tool for measuring air pressure.

Dropwindsonde (sonde): a small device dropped in the center of a hurricane to collect data such as air pressure, temperature, humidity, wind speed, and wind direction. The information helps forecasters track the storm.

Eye: the relatively calm, low-pressure center of a hurricane.

Eye wall: the ring of storm clouds surrounding the eye or center of a hurricane. The strongest winds and heaviest rains typically occur within the eye wall.

Figure 4: two passes made through a hurricane to collect data samples from four quadrants of a storm, such as north, south, east, and west.

Global Positioning System (GPS) dropwindsonde (sonde): a weather instrument released in the center of a hurricane's eye to collect information such as temperature, air pressure, and wind speed.

G-4 or Gulfstream-IV jet: a high-tech, high-speed aircraft that hurricane hunters fly around developing hurricanes.

Hurricane: a type of tropical cyclone—a low-pressure, spiraling storm system that develops in the tropics—with intense winds of seventy-four miles per hour or greater.

Hurricane hunters: people who fly into tropical cyclones, such as hurricanes, to collect weather information that will help predict the path of storms and keep the public safe.

Hurricane season: the most likely time of year for hurricanes to occur. In the Atlantic Ocean, the Gulf of Mexico, and the Central Pacific Ocean, the hurricane season is June 1 to November 30. In the Eastern Pacific Ocean, it's May 15 to November 30.

Meteorologist: a scientist who studies and forecasts weather.

National Oceanic and Atmospheric Administration (NOAA): a government agency that studies the earth's oceans and atmosphere and is responsible for tracking and forecasting dangerous weather. Its agencies include the National Weather Center and the National Hurricane Center.

P-3 or WP-3D Orion turboprop plane: a type of aircraft hurricane hunters fly directly into storms. The P-3s cruise at 345 miles per hour and allow scientists to collect storm data at altitudes of 1,500 to 25,000 feet.

Rain bands: curved stretches of thunderstorms projecting from the eye of a hurricane that sometimes spawn tornadoes.

Tropical cyclone: a general term for low-pressure, spiraling storm systems—such as tropical depressions, tropical storms, and hurricanes—that form over tropical waters. In the Northern Hemisphere, winds move counterclockwise. In the Southern Hemisphere, they move clockwise.

Tropical depression: a type of tropical cyclone with organized clouds and thunderstorms that have maximum sustained winds of thirty-eight miles or less per hour.

Tropical storm: a type of tropical cyclone containing strong thunderstorms and maximum sustained winds of thirty-nine to seventy-three miles per hour.

Typhoon: a hurricane that forms in the North Pacific Ocean or the China seas.

Wind shear: a sudden change in wind speed or direction—vertically or horizontally—along a plane's flight path.

Brad Lubbers (left) and Eric Banks ham it up before a Kentucky cave expedition. Having fun is always an important part of the journey, they say.

CAVE WOMAN

Calcite: a form of calcium carbonate.

Calcium carbonate: a mineral commonly found in rocks such as limestone.

Carbonic acid: a weak acid that forms when rainwater mixes with carbon dioxide.

Cave: a natural underground chamber or passage large enough for people to enter.

Caver: a person who explores caves.

Column: a calcite cave formation created when stalactites meet stalagmites.

DNA (Deoxyribonucleic acid): a molecule that carries and passes on genetic information.

Epigenic cave: a cave created by rainwater that seeps through cracks in the soil, turns into a weak acid, and eats away at the rock over thousands of years until channels and passages form.

Extremophiles: microbes that thrive in extreme environments, including those that are extremely hot, cold, or starved.

Helictites: cave formations that grow as small twisted structures projecting at different angles.

Limestone: rock made mostly of calcium carbonate and generally formed by the accrual of organic remains, such as shells. It's the primary rock found in caves worldwide.

Microbes: tiny life forms, such as bacteria, that can be seen only with a microscope.

Microbiologist: a scientist who studies microbes.

Mineral: an inorganic substance that's not a plant or animal.

Passage: a corridor created by water and rockfalls.

Pit: a vertical shaft formed by dripping or falling water through a crack.

Popcorn: a cave formation shaped like the snack.

Speleologist: a person who studies caves.

Speleothems: cave formations caused by mineral deposits.

Stalactite: a calcite cave formation that hangs down from the ceiling like an icicle.

Stalagmite: a calcite cave formation that reaches upward from the cave floor.

Troglobite: an animal that lives its entire life in a cave and adapts to total darkness.

Troglophile: an animal that can live in or out of a cave.

Some plants—called epiphytes—grow on trees without parasitizing or taking food from them. Redwood forests support a wide variety of epiphytes, such as these lichens and bryophytes (mosslike plants).

Botanist: a scientist who identifies and studies plants.

Cambium: the living tissue beneath the bark of a tree.

Canopy bonsai: small trees that grow at the tops of other trees such as redwoods.

Canopy soils: dirt made of decomposed foliage and debris that collects in redwood treetops over hundreds of years.

Crown: the upper (top) part of a tree.

Ecosystem: interaction of living things, such as plants and animals, within an environment, such as a forest or a tall-tree canopy.

Epiphytes: plants that grow on trees without parasitizing or taking food from them. Redwoods support a wide variety of epiphytes.

Eucalyptus regnans: scientific name for the world's tallest flowering plant. Australians call it mountain ash in Victoria and swamp gum in Tasmania.

Fire caves: chambers within redwoods and other trees hollowed out by fires over the centuries.

Forest canopy: the thick, leafy coverings formed by clusters of tall-tree crowns.

Laser range finder: a device for measuring the height of tall trees.

Leader: highest shoot on a tree.

Lichen: a unique organism resulting from a symbiotic relationship between fungus and algae

Mapping: measuring various parts of a tree so a three-dimensional computer model can be built and provide insights as to how the tree functions.

Old-growth (ancient) forests: biologically complex forests that have evolved naturally over hundreds of years.

Organism: a life form, such as a plant or animal.

Photosynthesis: how green plants chemically make food.

Reiterations: new, repeat versions of redwood trees that grow in response to damage to the main trunk.

Sensors: tools scientists install on treetops to measure environmental forces affecting trees, including temperature and humidity.

Sequoia sempervirens: scientific name for coast redwood trees—the tallest trees in the world.

Skywalking: a tree-climbing method that involves hanging in midair from a complex web of ropes hung on branches and moving about a crown without touching anything.

Tree boats: hammocks climbers stretch across branches to sleep in tall trees.

Widow-makers: unstable chunks of deadwood within a tree that can break loose and hit climbers as the chunks fall to the ground.

XYZ coordinates: three numbers representing a position point that are used to measure and map a tree.

SOURCE NOTES

HURRICANE HUNTER

Interviews with Paul Flaherty, meteorologist, flight director, and hurricane hunter for the National Oceanic and Atmospheric Administration (NOAA); and Lieutenant Junior Grade Rebecca J. Almeida. *Hurricanes . . . Unleashing Nature's Fury: A Preparedness Guide* by the U.S. Department of Commerce, the National Oceanic and Atmospheric Administration, and the National Weather Service, revised January 2007. NOAA at www.noaa.gov. National Weather Service at www.nhc.noaa.gov/index.shtml; Hurricane Hunters Association at www.hurricanehunters.com. 403rd Wing, United States Air Force Reserves, at www.403wg.afrc.af.mil. Jeffrey Masters, Ph.D., chief meteorologist at the Weather Underground, www.wunderground.com, and his online account of the near fatal NOAA Hurricane Hugo mission in September 1989.

CAVE WOMAN

Interviews with Hazel A. Barton, Ph.D., Ashland Endowed Professor of Integrative Science and assistant professor of biological sciences at Northern Kentucky University (NKU), Highland Heights, Kentucky; Dr. Norman R. Pace, director, Pace Laboratory, and professor in the department of Molecular, Cellular and Developmental Biology at the University of Colorado at Boulder; Brad Lubbers, Barton Research Group lab technician; and Eric Banks, undergraduate microbiology research student at NKU. Hazel Barton's Cave Science website at www.cavescience.com. "Combining Microbiology with Other Interests: Hobbies, Holes, and Hollywood," by Hazel Barton, *MicrobeLibrary* article: Focus on Microbiology Education, May 2005. "Cave Slime," by Stephen Hart, *Astrobiology Magazine: Search for Life in the Universe*, June 2003. "Introduction to

An enormous stalagmite called the White Giant catches Hazel's eye as she explores Carlsbad Caverns in New Mexico. Stalagmites, which are created by a buildup of minerals, project upward from a cave's floor.

Cave Microbiology: A Review for the Non-Specialist," by Hazel A. Barton, *Journal of Cave and Karst Studies* 68, no. 2 (August 2006): 43–54. *Life on Earth,* natural history television series, British Broadcasting Corporation (BBC One), 1979. *Journey into Amazing Caves,* MacGillivray Freeman Films, at www.amazingcaves.com. "Glossary of Cave Terms" National Park Service, U.S. Department of Interior, Mammoth Cave, at www.nps.gov/archive/maca/learnhome/glossary.htm.

Note: Nichol Creek Cave is a fictitious name given to a real cave in Kentucky that scientists are exploring. Landowners wish to keep the location secret to keep others from exploiting it.

SKYWALKER

Interview with Prof. Stephen C. Sillett, Kenneth L. Fisher Chair in Redwood Forest Ecology at Humboldt State University, Arcata, California. "Advancing the World's Understanding of Redwood Forest Ecology," website of Prof. Stephen Sillett at www.humboldt.edu/~sillett. "Climbing the Redwoods," by Richard Preston, *The New Yorker,* February 14 and 21, 2005. *The Wild Trees: A Story of Passion and Daring,* by Richard Preston (Random House, 2007). "Higher Learning," by Amy Leinbach Marquis, National Parks Conservation Association, *National Parks* magazine, spring 2006 (www.npca.org/magazine). "One for the Record Books," by Vernon Felton, photos by Kellie Jo Brown, "The Boldt: An Electronic Dispatch for Alumni and Friends of Humboldt State University," May 2007. Save-the-Redwoods League (www.savetheredwoods.org); "Interview: Gorge Koch and Steve Sillett discuss their research on the world's tallest trees," *Talk of the Nation/Science Friday,* National Public Radio, April 23, 2004.

TRAILBLAZING TERMS

Adapted from the National Weather Service National Hurricane Center Glossary of NHC Terms: www.nhc.noaa.gov/aboutgloss.shtml; *Hurricanes . . . Unleashing Nature's Fury: A Preparedness Guide* by the U.S. Department of Commerce, the National Oceanic and Atmospheric Administration, and the National Weather Service, revised January 2007; and "Glossary of Cave Terms," National Park Service, U.S. Department of Interior, Mammoth Cave, at www.nps.gov/archive/maca/learnhome/glossary.htm.

PHOTOGRAPHY CREDITS

Hurricane-hunting pilots employ courage and an array of flight instruments to carve through powerful storms.

INDEX